FOOD SAFETY

A TRUE BOOK

by

Joan Kalbacken

Children's Press®
A Division of Grolier Publishing
New York London Hong Kong Sydney
Danbury, Connecticut

Reading Consultant
Linda Cornwell
Learning Resource Consultant
Indiana Department
of Education

Visit Children's Press on the Internet at:
http://publishing.grolier.com

Library of Congress Cataloging-in-Publication Data

Kalbacken, Joan.
    Food safety / by Joan Kalbacken.
        p.   cm. — (A true book)
    Includes bibliographical references and index.
    Summary: Discusses various health concerns related to the foods we
eat and tells how to avoid them.
    ISBN: 0-516-20757-1 (lib. bdg.)   0-516-26377-3 (pbk.)
    1. Foodborne diseases—Juvenile literature.   2. Food handling—
Juvenile literature.   [1. Foodborne diseases.   2. Food handling.]
I. Title. II. Series.
RA601.5.K35   1998
615.9`54—dc21   97-8230
                                                                    CIP
                                                                    AC

Contents

Fruits, vegetables, and natural juices are especially important to your good health.

Food Sickness

Food is important for maintaining your growth and good health. But food carries germs called bacteria. Bacteria are very tiny living things that exist all around you and inside of you. They can only be seen with a microscope. Both good and bad bacteria can be

Bacteria give blue cheese (right) its greenish-blue color.

found in food. Some good bacteria produce yogurt, bread, and blue cheese. But bad bacteria can make you sick. Sickness caused by food bacteria is a big problem in the United States. Some scientists think that between 6

and 33 million people each
year get sick from the food
they eat.

Salmonella (sal-muh-NEL-
uh) are rod-shaped bacteria
that can cause sickness in

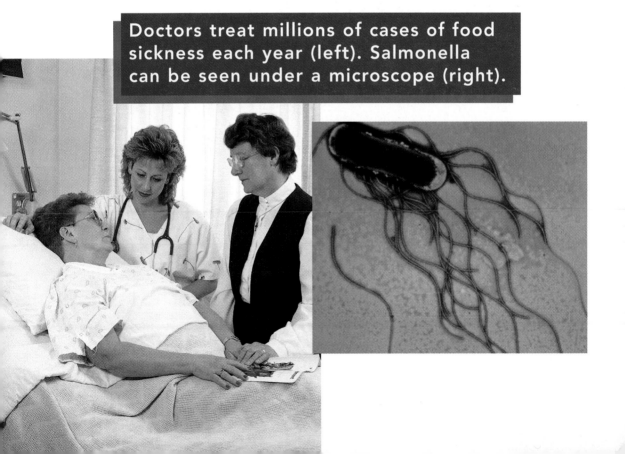

Doctors treat millions of cases of food
sickness each year (left). Salmonella
can be seen under a microscope (right).

people and animals. The first signs of salmonella sickness are headaches, chills, upset stomach, and weakness. Sometimes people mistake these signs for the flu.

Salmonella bacteria are carried in food. They can be found in raw meat, poultry (chickens, turkeys, ducks, and geese), and frozen, dried, or cracked eggs. The bacteria grow when food is left out on a table or countertop for a long time. It is impor-

Meat (top left) and cracked eggs (top right) are places where salmonella can grow. It's important to carefully wrap or cover food before storing it in the refrigerator (bottom).

tant to put meat products (such as sausage, bacon, beef, chicken, and some salads) into the refrigerator as soon as you are done eating.

Tiny worms are the source for trichinosis (left). Before you eat a pork chop (right), check to be sure it is fully cooked.

Trichinosis (trik-uh-NOH-siss) is caused by tiny worms that are found in pork that has not been fully cooked. If pork is not cooked properly, the worms grow and multiply inside you after you've eaten. It sometimes takes several days or weeks before the sickness starts. Vomiting, sweating, chills, and weakness are some of the signs of trichinosis sickness. In order to keep from getting sick, every part of the meat must be thoroughly cooked. This means that there is no red or pink color when you cut into it. Pork may be kept frozen, but it should never be kept for more than thirty days.

The most common food sickness is staphylococcus (staff-uh-luh-KAHK-uhs). It is usually called by its nickname, "staph." Many people get sick from staph, but do not know it. As a result, no one knows exactly how many people get sick from staph each year. Stomachaches, nausea, and headaches are common with a staph sickness. It usually lasts only a day or two, so most people think it is the flu.

It can be hard to tell the difference between the flu and a staph sickness. Staph sicknesses occur so often because the bacteria that cause it (inset) are found everywhere.

Staph bacteria are found on most animals. Even humans carry them on their skin. Staph are usually not harmful, unless they are passed along to someone else on food. If you touch a person's food with dirty hands, you might cause that person to get sick. This is why it is important to wash your hands. Some of the foods that you can easily catch a staph sickness from

Touching food with dirty hands can cause staph to be passed on to other people.

Cream-filled bakery items (left) can contain staph bacteria. Products made with milk (right) can also be sources of staph bacteria.

are cream-filled bakery goods, ham, poultry, and milk products.

A few people get very sick with staph, so it can be a dangerous sickness. But most people are not affected seriously.

How to Avoid Food Sickness

You can stop harmful bacteria from growing by keeping cold food cold and hot food hot. The temperature Danger Zone is from 40 degrees Fahrenheit (4 degrees Celsius) to 140 degrees Fahrenheit (60 degrees Celsius). It is called the Danger

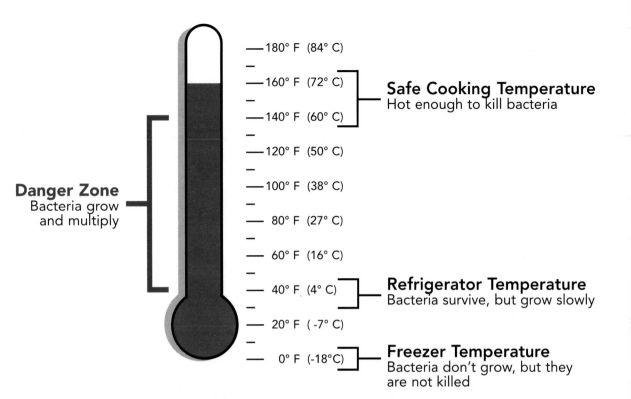

—180° F (84° C)
—
—160° F (72° C)   **Safe Cooking Temperature**
—   Hot enough to kill bacteria
—140° F (60° C)
—
—120° F (50° C)
—
—100° F (38° C)
—
— 80° F (27° C)
—
— 60° F (16° C)
—
— 40° F (4° C)   **Refrigerator Temperature**
—   Bacteria survive, but grow slowly
— 20° F (-7° C)
—
— 0° F (-18°C)   **Freezer Temperature**
                   Bacteria don't grow, but they
                   are not killed

Danger Zone
Bacteria grow
and multiply

The Danger Zone includes the temperatures at which bacteria grow quickly.

Zone because harmful bacteria grow best between these temperatures. Meat, fish, eggs, poultry, fresh vegetables, and

dairy foods should be stored below 40 degrees Fahrenheit (4 degrees Celsius). If these foods are kept within the Danger Zone (for example, at an outdoor summer picnic) for more than two hours, they could be unsafe to eat.

Bacteria are not killed when foods are kept below 40 degrees Fahrenheit (4 degrees Celsius). They grow very slowly. So foods can be unsafe if they are kept too long in the refrigerator. Many foods should not stay in the refrigerator for more than three days.

To kill most harmful bacteria, food should be cooked above 160 degrees Fahrenheit (72

How Can You Tell if Food is Unsafe?

Signs of unsafe food include mold on the food, unusual color, or unusual smell. But sometimes it's hard to tell if food is not safe by just looking at it. You should never taste food to see if it tastes bad. Never feed possibly unsafe food to pets. Pets can become sick, too. If you are not sure about the safety of a food, throw it out.

Food that has grown mold, such as this grapefruit and bread should be thrown into the garbage immediately.

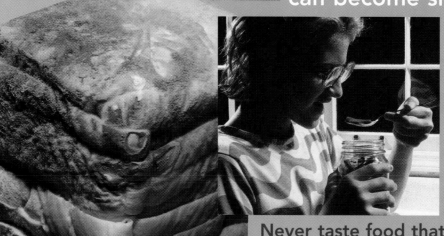

Never taste food that you think might be bad.

MICROWAVE POP

1 **POP** Unfold one popcorn bag and place in center of oven with INSTRUCTION SIDE UP. Using full power (HIGH) set timer for 5 minutes. Popping time may take as few as 2 minutes or as many as 5 minutes because microwave ovens vary. **DO NOT LEAVE MICROWAVE UNATTENDED WHILE POPPING.**

Follow the cooking instructions for all foods, especially foods that are cooked in a microwave.

degrees Celsius). When you use a microwave oven, be sure to follow instructions on the food's packaging carefully. Food containers should be turned inside the microwave to be sure that all the food is cooked correctly. All of the microwaved food must be hot. But be careful! Food must be hot enough to kill bacteria, but you can be badly burned by the steam or the heat of the food. Be sure an adult is present before you microwave any food.

Proper handwashing fights bacteria, too. Everything you touch has bacteria on it. Remember that when you touch food with unclean hands you get bacteria on

Never touch food without first washing your hands.

your food. This can cause the food to be unsafe to eat. Before you touch any food, wash your hands with soap and warm water. Count to twenty before you finish washing.

People who handle food in restaurants often wear gloves to keep from spreading bacteria to customers.

Any food handling should begin with clean hands, clean cooking tools, and clean work areas (tables or countertops). In fact, many people who work with food in restaurants wear gloves. This helps to ensure that others are eating safe food.

Fresh fruits and vegetables are good for you. But unwashed fruits and vegetables can carry bacteria. These foods can be made safe by washing them in plenty of cold, clean water.

Washing fruits and vegetables in cold water is the best way to remove dirt and bacteria.

Food Safety Laws

The United States is one of the safest countries in the world for good, healthy food. The U.S. government has been concerned about safe food for many years. President Theodore Roosevelt (1901–09) signed the first food and drug act in 1906. The act made sure

Food that is shipped into and out of the United States is among the safest in the world.

that all food and medicine meet safety rules. Since then, government agencies have

This scientist at the Food and Drug Administration is looking for ways to improve food safety.

been formed to assure food safety in this country. The Food and Drug Administration (FDA) makes sure that the food laws are obeyed. The

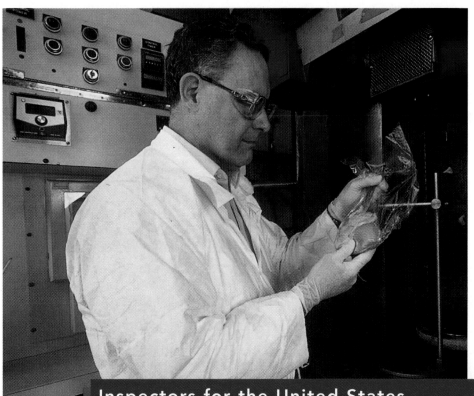

Inspectors for the United States Department of Agriculture check food to make sure it is safe for people to eat.

United States Department of Agriculture (USDA) inspects all meat or poultry shipped into the United States.

Food Labels

Food labels carry warnings about the safety of food products. All of the ingredients in the food must be listed on the label. The label must also list the name and address of the company that made the food. Many labels have instructions about the safe handling of

SELL BY
03-26-97

****TOTAL PRICE****
$3.90

NET WT./COUNT
1.15 lb

UNIT PRICE
$3.39

SAFE HANDLING INSTRUCTIONS

THIS PRODUCT WAS PREPARED FROM INSPECTED AND PASSED MEAT AND/OR POULTRY. SOME FOOD PRODUCTS MAY CONTAIN BACTERIA THAT COULD CAUSE ILLNESS IF THE PRODUCT IS MISHANDLED OR COOKED IMPROPERLY. FOR YOUR PROTECTION, FOLLOW THESE SAFE HANDLING INSTRUCTIONS.

KEEP REFRIGERATED OR FROZEN. THAW IN REFRIGERATOR OR MICROWAVE.

KEEP RAW MEAT AND POULTRY SEPARATE FROM OTHER FOODS. WASH WORKING SURFACES (INCLUDING CUTTING BOARDS), UTENSILS, AND HANDS AFTER TOUCHING RAW MEAT OR POULTRY.

COOK THOROUGHLY.

KEEP HOT FOODS HOT. REFRIGERATE LEFTOVERS IMMEDIATELY OR DISCARD.

Meat labels remind users to store the food properly, to wash your hands before touching it, and to cook it properly.

food. For example, meat labels instruct users to keep the meat refrigerated or frozen. The labels also suggest that raw meat and poultry

31

Keeping your kitchen and dishes clean is an important part of food safety.

should be kept separate from other foods. Some labels even carry reminders that cutting boards and countertops should be washed thoroughly.

Labels also tell us that a food should be sold or cooked by a certain date. The food may not be safe after the date listed.

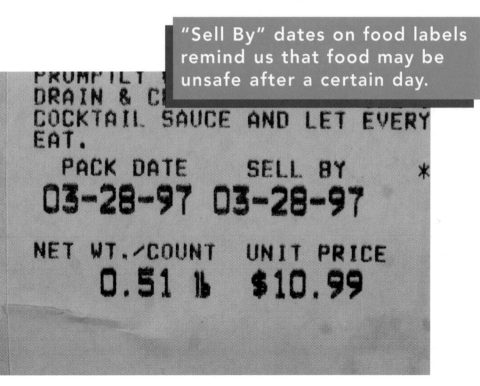

"Sell By" dates on food labels remind us that food may be unsafe after a certain day.

Chemicals in Food

Insects can carry bacteria into food. Chemicals are used to kill insects that might damage our food. They are also used by farmers to help grow some of the food we eat. Farmers can only use certain types of chemicals. A part of the government called the

Spraying chemicals on crops from an airplane is called crop dusting.

Environmental Protection Agency (EPA) tells farmers which chemicals are safe to use and how much of them to use.

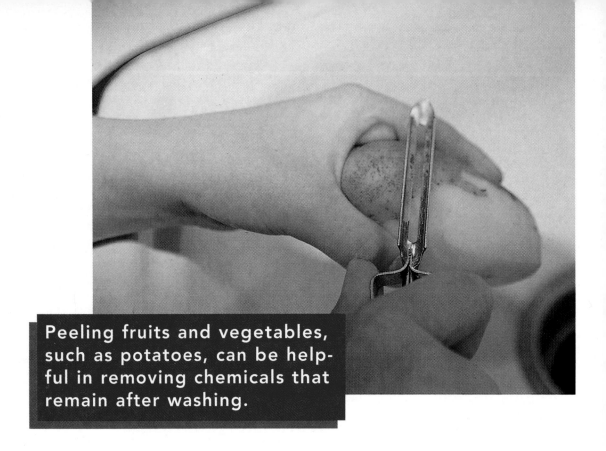

Peeling fruits and vegetables, such as potatoes, can be helpful in removing chemicals that remain after washing.

To help get rid of any chemicals left on fruits or vegetables, wash and peel them before you eat. Removing the outer leaves of lettuce, spinach, and other leafy foods can also help.

Food Allergies

An allergy is an unpleasant reaction to certain foods. The signs of an allergy might be hives (welts), swelling of the face or hands, itching, shortness of breath, or difficulty swallowing. The foods most likely to cause a serious reaction include peanuts, milk, eggs, and shellfish (crabs, lobsters, or shrimp). It's important to call a doctor or a poison control center immediately if you have a bad reaction to something that you eat.

A test for allergies

Shellfish are a common source of food allergies.

The Food Safety Team

Food safety depends on many people. The members of a food safety team include government officials, farmers or growers, food makers, food sellers, and customers (people who buy the food). Government officials make food safety laws and make

Food safety begins on the farms or fields on which food is grown (above). Most of the food that can be found in grocery stores has been packaged according to strict government laws (right).

sure the laws are being obeyed. Farmers and growers use safe amounts of chemicals to get rid of insects and bacteria. Food makers package and label foods according to

Grocery store customers who look for clean, undamaged food products are important members of the food safety team.

government rules. Food sellers keep food safe in the stores until it is bought. And customers buy the safe food and store it and cook it properly.

You can be a member of the food safety team, too. Here are some food safety rules to help keep you and others from getting a food sickness:

1. Keep hot food hot and cold food cold.

2. Wash your hands with warm, soapy water before you touch any food.

3. Use clean dishes, spoons, forks, and knives.

4. Wash fresh fruits and vegetables with cold, clean water.

Learning food safety rules will help to keep you and others safe from food sicknesses.

5. Don't put your school-books or other belongings on the counter or table when food is out.

6. If you think food is unsafe, throw it out.

7. Look for a warning on food labels to use food by a certain date.

8. Microwave food carefully. Follow the package instructions. Always have an adult present to help you.

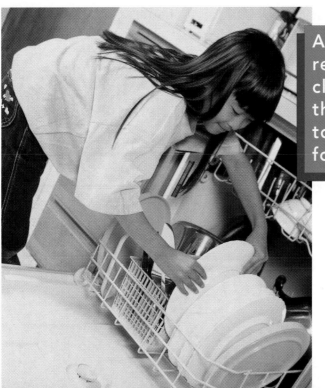

Always remember that cleanliness is the best way to keep food safe.

To Find Out More

Here are some additional resources to help you learn more about food sicknesses, allergies, and food safety:

 **Books**

Davis, Kay and Wendy Oldsfield. **Food.** Raintree Steck-Vaughn, 1991.

Kalbacken, Joan. **The Food Pyramid.** Children's Press, 1998.

Kalbacken, Joan. **Vitamins and Minerals.** Children's Press, 1998.

Patten, Barbara. **Food Safety.** Rourke, 1995.

Seixas, Judith. **Allergies— What They Are, What They Do.** Greenwillow, 1991.

Stille, Darlene R. **The Digestive System.** Children's Press, 1997.

Organizations and Online Sites

Department of Health and Human Services (DHHS)
200 Independence Ave. SW
Washington, DC 20201
http://www.os.dhhs.gov/

The United States's main agency for protecting the health of all Americans and providing services such as medical research, disease prevention, food and drug safety, and more.

Food and Drug Administration (FDA)
5600 Fishers Lane
Rockville, MD 20857
http://www.fda.gov/

This government agency works to protect the health of the American people by making sure that food is safe, healthy, and clean.

KidsHealth
http://www.kidshealth.org/

Created by medical experts, this site is devoted entirely to the health of children. Contains accurate, up-to-date information about growth, food, fitness, health games, animations, the KidsVote health poll, and lots of surprises!

United States Department of Agriculture (USDA)
14th Street and
  Independence Avenue SW
Washington, DC 20250
*http://www.nal.usda.gov/
fnic/Fpyr/pyramid.html*

This is a group of federal agencies that work to ensure food safety and nutrition, to support American farming, and to conserve our country's natural resources and the environment.

45

Important Words

assure to promise something or to make certain

handling touching with the hands

harmful something that can injure or hurt you (or someone else)

inspect to look at something very carefully

microscope instrument that makes very small things look large

mold growth on the surface of food, a type of decay

multiply to grow in number or amount

nausea a feeling of being sick to your stomach

Index

Meet the Author

Joan Kalbacken lives in Normal, Illinois. A former teacher, she taught mathematics and French for twenty-nine years. Ms. Kalbacken is the author of several books for Children's Press, including *The Food Pyramid* and *Vitamins and Minerals*, companion books to *Food Safety*. Ms. Kalbacken is also the recipient of a Distinguished Illinois Author Award from the Illinois Reading Council, and a Merit Teaching Award from the Illinois Those Who Excel Program.